HEART'S HEALING

COMFORTING WORDS
ABOUT LIFE AFTER DEATH
A Medium Speaks to Hospice Workers

Also from Mastery Press:

Mastery Press

The Spirit World, Where Love Reigns Supreme

The Blue Island
Beyond Titanic—Voyage into Spirit

The Hum of Heaven

The Wisdom of Saint Germain

The Gift of Mediumship

Awaken the Sleeping Giant

A Legacy of Love
Volume One: The Return to Mount Shasta and Beyond

To Master Self is to Master Life

A Wanderer in the Spirit Lands

HEART'S HEALING

COMFORTING WORDS ABOUT LIFE AFTER DEATH
A Medium Speaks to Hospice Workers

PHILIP BURLEY

Mastery Press

Phoenix, Arizona

Copyright © 2010 by Philip Burley

Published by:

Mastery Press

A division of
Adventures in Mastery (AIM), LLC

All rights reserved. No part of this book may be reproduced
in any form or by any means, electronic or mechanical,
including photocopying, recording, or by any information
storage or retrieval system without permission in writing
from the publishers. Inquiries should be addressed to:

Mastery Press
P.O. Box 43548
Phoenix, AZ 85080
PB@PhilipBurley.com

ISBN: 978-1-883389-18-5
eISBN: 978-1-883389-30-7

Printed in the United States of America

Cover and interior design
by 1106 Design, Phoenix, Arizona

Dedication

For hospice workers and their patients.

Acknowledgments

I want to express my heartfelt appreciation to everyone who helped bring this book into existence, especially my wife Vivien, who increased my awareness of hospice services through her years as a volunteer with Hospice of the Valley. I'm very grateful to my long-time friend Ron O'Keefe, who gave his valuable time and attention to the initial review and editing of this work; and my enduring thanks go to my assistant, Lynn Mathers for her careful and competent attention to the many details associated with getting the book to press.

I'm fortunate indeed that my editor, Anne Edwards, worked closely with hospice staff and patients for many years, both as a nursing home clinical social worker and director of community services for the elderly. Her sensitive contributions to this book reflect not only her editing skills, but her intimate experience with those approaching life's end, and her special respect for hospice work.

I remain deeply appreciative of the work of the hospice staff and volunteers whose questions prompted the contents of this book. I'm especially grateful to Sue Leach, former Volunteer Coordinator for Scottsdale Memorial Hospice and Hospice of the Valley, in Phoenix, Arizona, for her friendship and example of service to others. In a recent conversation, Sue reflected on her fifteen years with hospice as the most meaningful work she has ever done, saying, "Each person's passing was a holy event. We were standing on sacred ground." Sue's words were similar to those I have heard from others who work with hospice patients and families.

As always, my gratitude flows unceasingly to those loving and wise beings in the world unseen who have guided my efforts for so long. Without them, my work and this book would not be possible.

Contents

Preface	xi
Foreword	xiii
Hospice and Life after Death	1
Do Dying People See Spirit Beings?	13
How Does Grief Affect Us and Loved Ones in Spirit?	21
What Are Near Death Experiences?	33
Can We Use Our Spiritual Senses to Understand Others?	41
How Can We Deal with Fear and Negativity?	51
Does Meditation Help?	67
What is Mediumship All About?	77
What Happens During a Spiritual Reading?	87
How Can We Know What Messages to Trust?	107
A Note on Hospice	113

Preface

Heart's Healing is based on transcripts of two presentations I was invited to give to volunteers of Scottsdale Memorial Hospice at Scottsdale Memorial Hospital, Scottsdale, Arizona in 1995 and 1996. The content has been edited for clarity and updated to include current information.

My wife Vivien volunteered for hospice for several years, and during the ordinary course of conversation with colleagues, shared information about my work as a professional medium. When I was subsequently asked to speak to hospice workers, we invited their questions on the relationship between life after death and their experiences with the dying. They wanted to know as many details as possible about the spirit world and what happens to us at the moment of physical death.

The depth and variety of questions asked by the hospice workers told me they already knew a great deal about the unique spiritual experiences of the dying. They knew firsthand what people see, hear, and sense near the end of life. From the beginning, people asked questions that were not about whether there is a life beyond this one, but about how to help their patients release fears of death and gain confidence in the continuity of life.

These loving, serving people were eager for information about the spirit world, because they have seen how important this reality has been to the experience of their patients. They work with those whose lives are replete with near death encounters! It was a privilege to spend time with people so dedicated to the comfort and care of others. I found them more sensitive than most to the many possibilities surrounding the next world, and I'm very happy to share with you our meaningful exchanges.

— Philip Burley

Foreword

By the late 1980s, more than fifteen years after we married, Philip was inspired to become a full time professional medium. He had been open to the world of spirit since childhood, but for many years was uncertain of the exact nature of his gift and how to develop it. Because we wanted to provide a serious and useful personal service, we enrolled in three years of study to gain a systematic understanding of the spirit world, and we spent much time doing practical exercises to open our spiritual senses. Since then, Philip has written books, taught meditation, spoken before numerous audiences, and provided spiritual readings and consultations for people all over the world. He also conducts a nationwide prayer service project. His reputation

Heart's Healing

as a medium has grown primarily by word of mouth, and he rarely advertises his work.

In the interval since our formal study of mediumship, I have worked as a case manager for disabled children and older adults and as a volunteer for Hospice of the Valley in Phoenix. My hospice work was a true highlight of my experience, as I served with people who provide patients and families with an excellent standard of physical, emotional, and spiritual care.

During the years I spent among hospice workers, I frequently heard them speak about experiences related to life after death, so it was natural for me to tell them about Philip's work. They were eager to hear what he had to say, and invited him to speak on two occasions. He came without prepared talks, because he sensed that my co-workers would need no prompting to ask questions about the spirit world. We are happy to share this rare insight into the spiritual experiences of the dying as witnessed by hospice workers, and to give you a look through Philip's unique window into a world that is the "next stop" for all of us.

— Vivien Burley

HEART'S HEALING

Hospice and Life after Death
Philip Burley Speaks to Hospice Workers

The spirit world will feel like home to us because we are spiritual beings...

Before we start with your questions, I want to thank you for the special work that you do. As hospice workers, you use your professional training, your hands and feet, and your heart and soul in service to others. You care for your patients with sensitivity and kindness at a uniquely important time in their lives—when they are preparing to part with people and things they love dearly, and when their bodies are simply giving out. Physical death is not always an easy process, but you are there, where and when you are most needed.

You also provide support and comfort to families of your patients with honesty, respect, and affection. If they can talk to anyone about what's *really* going on, I'm sure it's you. You are the ones who care before, during, and after families experience the loss of someone dearly beloved. Again, it's not easy, and feelings are sometimes complicated, but you are there.

I know something about your work from what Vivien has shared, and I certainly am aware of your fine reputation. But I know the most essential thing about you from my own experience with what we call death and its impact on the human soul. Like you, I support and counsel people who have lost a loved one, and like you, I serve those who are near death—though they're often on the other side of the experience!

If there is one word most likely to sum up the feelings of patients, families, the community, and many in the world of spirit when they think of you, that word would have to be *gratitude*.

※ ※

When I speak, I don't like to assume that I already know your concerns, and I don't wish to speak on topics that don't interest you. It would help me greatly to know your questions. Let's begin!

Question: *Have you ever counseled a hospice patient or family member about life after death?*

Hospice and Life after Death

Philip: Before I became a professional medium, I spoke to various groups across the United States on the reality of the spirit world, based on my spiritual experiences and independent study. My first encounter with a hospice patient was in Dallas, Texas, while I was there to give one of these talks.

A friend in Dallas who was doing hospice work got a phone call from an acquaintance who said that a dying patient admitted to the Dallas Memorial Hospital urgently needed to speak with someone about spiritual matters. My friend asked me to rush over to the hospital with him to see this man. When I agreed to go, he picked me up and drove like crazy, thinking the man might pass on at any moment. When we got to the hospital, the hospice patient was sitting up in bed, wide awake. His *wife*, however, was sitting at the foot of his bed, reclining against the wall, fast asleep.

I sat down in a chair next to the bed, introduced myself, and said to the hospice patient, "They told me that you were close to passing." He replied, "Well, last night I *felt* that way. I had no idea what was happening. I was dozing off to sleep, and my wife was sitting by my side as you are now, also beginning to nod. She told me she was startled awake when I suddenly yelled out, 'Take my hand! Take my hand! I'm going out of my body, and I'm going to hit the ceiling!'" He went on to tell me he did indeed rise up to the ceiling, from where he could see his body below. This is what frightened him, and he called out to his wife in distress.

This gentleman was very confused by his experience, and felt fear based on a sense that he was losing control of his mind or his body, or both, and he was very anxious about what might be next. I explained that he was already a spiritual being inside his physical body, and because his body was deteriorating, his spirit was becoming freer. What he had experienced was his spirit actually rising out of his body, though it remained attached to his physical form. His fear that he might hit the ceiling was caused by his spirit's rising to that level, making it possible to look down and see his body in the bed below. I let him know that others had experienced similar episodes and had actually risen through the ceiling, none the worse for wear!

I explained that the time would come when he was likely to find himself rising from his body not to return, and told him we will all go through the same process, though details may vary, because it's part of natural or spiritual law. I assured him that this normal part of everyone's life is similar to the process of birth, but usually much easier!

I shared my understanding, in simple terms, with this hospitalized hospice patient as his wife slept. He became visibly more relaxed as we spoke. He asked several questions, and we spent the better part of an hour together before we said goodnight.

Question: Can you tell us more about what happens to us just before and right after we die?

Philip: You've just heard that people may have out of body experiences before dying, though we can have these experiences at any time in our lives, especially when we are sleeping. Some patients near death get a strong sense that it's "time to go," but they don't know where and don't realize they are feeling the spirit pulling away from the body. Others hear voices or music or see faces of angels or relatives. I'm sure some of you have witnessed such episodes as you do your work.

I don't know what happens if the person is in a final sleep or coma when they pass over, but I can imagine that they experience dying almost as though they are in a dream state. That must be a beautiful experience, and it may be quite seamless, with no physical discomfort at all. It's anxiety that tends to increase or even cause physical discomfort, and that's not an issue if we pass over while sleeping.

What happens just *after* physical death is my area of greater expertise. Most who have had near death experiences testify there is great beauty, much light, and a gathering of loved ones waiting for us just on the other side. Knowing we are coming, our loved ones have prepared for us, and there is really nothing for us to fear. On the contrary, there is every reason to have hope, faith, and trust that our lives are about to get better!

We are leaving behind every ache and pain, every unwanted wrinkle, and all discomfort associated with our physical lives. We are saying goodbye to old age, financial worries, any leaks we might have in the roof, car trouble, and other physical or practical problems and stepping into a world that we will immediately recognize, though it is more beautiful than we can imagine.

The spirit world will feel like home to us because we are spiritual beings who already live "there," even as we go through the challenges of this physical life. We just can't see our spiritual surroundings with our physical eyes. We find beauty and peace in contemplation because, through the stillness, we touch the spiritual reality we are destined to experience fully at the moment of death.

I have read in many sources that people who have long illness or disability may need a period of recuperation in the spirit world when the physical body dies. Even though they leave their illnesses and disabilities behind, their mental states may be fixed on the idea of being disabled or ill. After a period of spiritual rehabilitation with spirit beings who have expertise in helping them feel rejuvenated, they experience their new lives in a place of greater beauty and love than we know on earth. This, of course, assumes that they have lived a good and loving life.

Question: *Hospice provides comfort care for the terminally ill, and we don't usually work with patients seeking aggressive treatment to prolong life. What do you think of this concept?*

Philip: As I'm sure you discuss in your initial training, death comes to all of us, and there may be a point in the course of any terminal illness where someone chooses to emphasize quality rather than quantity of life. This physical life is very valuable because we enrich the lives of others, and we grow throughout life's experiences, but we all have a time to go. When someone is ready to step into the next world, you are the earth angels who work in tandem with spiritual angels to help someone go through the transition.

Question: *Since hospice patients represent so many different religious backgrounds, and we also* *encounter agnostics and atheists, what is our best approach to the subject of life after death?*

Philip: I'm sure you have guidelines and policies to follow, but generally speaking, I recommend listening to your patients' stories about their beliefs if they are willing to share these, and asking follow up questions to see if you can get a discussion going. Patients may be more than eager to share, since life after death has become of immediate interest to many of them. It certainly was to the hospice patient I met in Texas.

The key is not to debate or convince, but to love. Listen with your heart, and respond to whatever you hear with kindness. You might want to use language to indicate you're sharing your own point of view, suggesting that when it's your turn, you're going to look for a trusted friend or loved one who has passed over before you, and you're going to look for a bright light.

Just this much information will give people something to do if they pass over and find themselves feeling confused, alone, or in darkness. Those who have no understanding at all about the spirit world have the greatest risk of this happening to them. Because you are giving such good care and you're motivated to serve, you are in a position of great trust with patients and families. Just be honest and respect all points of view, as I'm sure you do.

If someone won't entertain the possibility of surviving death, and doesn't want to talk about it, there's not much to do; but you can try speaking in terms of a bet or a joke. I have a friend who tells her agnostic sister, "When we meet in the spirit world, we'll talk it over again." Hospice is one of the few agencies providing care that includes spiritual counseling and support for patients, and that's a wonderful service. You might ask one of your chaplains for advice. If you are working closely with a patient, it's good to have an approach in mind.

Do Dying People See Spirit Beings?

If people knew the reality of spirit world and the process of leaving the physical body, they could die without fear. They would realize they are about to gather again with those they loved on earth and meet ancestors they never knew.

Question: *I have been around dying people who seem to communicate with unseen others, sometimes nodding, smiling, or even speaking to them. Can you explain what is happening?*

Philip: You are privileged in your work to witness what it is like to leave this physical world. You have seen all the motions people go through, moving, grimacing, moaning, or talking to unseen visitors. Even though death scenes in movies show people dying in pain, there is usually little pain in the actual process. What we are looking at is the spirit naturally seeking release from the body, and clairvoyants can actually see the spirit leaving the body at the moment of physical death. Have any of you seen a light or some kind of energy around a patient who is passing over? *[From various audience members: Yes.]*

A dying person is more out of the body than in. If you could see such a person clairvoyantly, you would probably see the spirit hovering above the physical body, or maybe off to the side, growing less and less cognizant of the physical world and more aware of the spiritual world. By the creator's very invention, we begin to put this world behind us as we move into the spirit world.

How many of you have had patients or relatives who said they saw people as they were about to die? *[Many positive responses.]* Some scientists say this is caused by certain changes in dying brain cells. When oxygen is reduced, some say, dying persons get more carbon dioxide, causing them to hallucinate. Perhaps changes in the brain of a dying person enhance the spiritual senses! Whatever the case, as the dying move away from their physical bodies into the spiritual world, they can see and hear things that are invisible and inaudible to us.

I'm sure you've noticed that breathing in people about to pass over grows very shallow. As they begin to separate from the physical body, they are beginning to breathe the atmosphere of the spiritual world they are preparing to enter.

The process is beautiful when you are aware of everything that is happening. Birth *into* this world is not without effort and struggle, as we know, yet we regard it a precious miracle. Our birth into the spirit world is equally precious, but we haven't valued it in the same way because we haven't understood what is going on.

If you understand the process of dying in the larger context of the spirit world, you are better able to assist patients to make a positive transition. If people knew the reality of spirit world and the process of leaving the physical body, they could die without fear. They would realize they are about to gather again with those they loved on earth and meet ancestors they never knew. What a great reunion! I've visited the spirit world in dreams or while out of my body, and I've seen the environment and spoken with the people there. Because of these experiences and the understanding I have, I'm not afraid of leaving my body and going to that world when it's time for me to do that.

When we pass into the spirit world, not only do we meet loved ones waiting on the other side, we have new opportunities to learn and grow. If

Heart's Healing

we have been ill, we gradually gain a wonderful sense of well-being. We have wholesome spiritual bodies corresponding exactly to our physical bodies, except that they are completely well, and we are in our prime. Beauty, by the way, is determined in the spirit world by the quality of love we bring into that sphere, not according to the standards we have in this life.

In the spirit world, we generally have heightened awareness, greater creativity, refined appreciation of beauty, and a deeper understanding of life. When we play the piano on earth, for example, our eye must see a note and send its image to the brain before the impulse comes back to our finger to press a piano key. In the world of spirit, we *are* our thoughts, so when we see a note, we play it. There is no time between seeing and doing. There is no earthly time at all in the world of spirit.

Comment: *Sometimes a dying person's face is so radiant that I know my patient has made contact with the other side. When I see this, I say something to encourage the person to keep going in that direction. It only takes a moment to have an important* *conversation and allow my patient to share what is happening.*

Philip: You're showing much wisdom and common sense. Have any of you seen your patients reaching up toward someone when they are near the moment of passing or heard them say something like, "My mother is here"? *[Many positive responses.]* Your work is beautiful, and you must enjoy it thoroughly!

Comment: *When I first began with hospice, friends would make a face and say, "How can you do that sort of work?" I never had a good answer except to say, "I enjoy it, and it's what I choose to do." Now, if that happens, I can say, "It's wonderful! I'm with people on a journey, and sometimes I want to go with them!"*

Question: *I was with my grandmother before she died, and she talked about times when she was a child, going back and forth between now and then, and about people waiting for her on the other side. She said she wasn't ready to go with them, and that she would go when she was ready! She was a* *stubborn lady! Is there is a way to know whether she was really seeing spirits or just going back in time in her memory?*

Philip: We can learn much from what a dying person has to say. The surfacing of memories and the ability to see beings in the spirit world can happen at the same time, and when people are in the process of dying, it doesn't matter which is true at any given moment. As long as what is happening is positive for patients, it's good to support and validate their experiences and not try to correct them. Let them have their visions of loved ones, real or imaginary. Everything happening is provided by providence for them, to help them make this transition.

How Does Grief Affect Us and Loved Ones in Spirit?

*Rising up from the earthly body
and moving into the greater
light of life is in accordance
with natural spiritual law...*

Question: *When we grieve for loved ones who have passed on, are we helping to bridge the gap between this world and the next, or are we hindering their passage to the other side?*

Philip: To lose someone we love is painful, no matter how much we understand and attune ourselves to the spirit world. We often feel lost and alone, and grieving is natural and necessary. After a time, most of us regain our sense of well-being in the absence of the one who has died. We miss the physical presence of our loved one, and our lives have changed, but we move on.

Can grief hold back the spirit of a loved one? It's a matter of degree and duration. We must not try to keep a loved one bound to earth to comfort us in our unremitting sorrow. What's important is to strike a balance, honoring our sad feelings, but not obsessing about someone who has died, any more than we would if that person were physically alive. Excessive grieving is akin to holding a baby in the birth canal beyond its time to be born. Rising up from the earthly body and moving into the greater light of life is in accordance with natural spiritual law, and we should understand and respect the new reality our loved one is experiencing. It is comforting to know our loved ones who have passed on are very much alive in a higher, finer dimension of existence.

After a period of adjustment, our loved ones can and will visit us many times in spirit because of the bond of love they share with us. While we no longer have the physical closeness we once had, we can have even greater closeness in heart. After our initial shock of loss and an adjustment period for our loved one in spirit, the relationship can find its own new normalcy. It's fine to express affection and appreciation, ask for advice, or even share a joke, just as you always have. You may find that your relationship continues to evolve and grow, as you move forward with your own life on earth, and your loved one moves forward in the spiritual dimension.

When we are deeply affected by grief, our spiritual senses may be more open than usual, and we become acutely aware of the presence of our loved one who has passed into the spirit world. We may have bedside visitations when we are drifting off to sleep or just waking up in the morning or have vivid dreams in which we experience a strong sense that we have actually been with our loved one.

Question: After my mother's death, I could see her and communicate with her, but my dad was distraught because he could never reach the point where he felt any contact with her. What can you do for people who seem unable to make contact with a loved one in the spirit world?

Philip: People in that situation often feel cheated, especially when they have been close to the person who has died. They want the contact desperately, but it doesn't happen for them.

I did one reading for a woman who wanted desperately to hear from a deceased loved one. She was a PhD psychologist associated with the Veteran's Administration Hospital near

Philadelphia, and in her case, I could clearly see that someone very close to her had died. When I asked her about this, she began to cry, and her husband came in from the spirit world. During the reading, he gave her evidential information that I couldn't have known.

The messages given by this woman's husband related specifically to her situation: I told her, "He wants you to get the rest of his clothes out of the house. You haven't gotten rid of all of them because of your grieving." I gave her another message from him about issues relating to their finances. She had been trying to resolve them, but she was still having trouble. Without knowing this, I told her that her husband was aware of the financial problem she was having and that it would be solved. A colleague of this woman later told me that the reading had changed her life. She was no longer showing her grief so openly around the hospital.

One of the best things you can do to help those who are grieving is to give them good literature to read about the spirit world—not superficial material on psychic phenomena, but literature that explains what happens when people die. Many of the books about "The Light" provide good information, or at least suggest the reality of the spirit world. Also, encourage someone who is grieving to consult with a medium if you find one with a good reputation, or get a referral from someone you trust. It is hard to find a really good medium, but they are out there.

Vivien: If someone yearns to be in touch with a departed loved one but is not having that experience, it could be because of stress and tension. Encourage the person to relax, because spiritual contact often comes when you are just open to the possibility but not necessarily expecting it. Another idea is for people who have lost a loved one to attend a meditation class. Meditation helps us learn how to be more aware of contact from the other side.

Philip: Because all of you are concerned with the grieving process, I want to share excerpts from letters I received from those who lost a loved one. Here is one from a woman who came for a reading after her husband died:

Dear Philip,

I know that you remember me. For some reason you have been constantly on my mind. I want to thank you again for your reading. My husband's death still haunts me after ten years, but your tape and reading have helped to heal so much. My husband still comes to me from the other side every time I go to a movie, just as you said he would. [I had told her in the reading that her husband loves movies and was often present when she went to one. She had confirmed he had always been a movie buff.]

I feel his presence whenever I get a chill. It runs up the back of my neck, just as you said it would. [Her husband had appeared in the reading and touched her in this way. Spirits do touch in with you through your nervous system.] You have no idea what a comfort it is to know he is still in my life.

The writer of this letter took all of our classes and opened up spiritually to the extent she could communicate directly with her husband in the spirit world. She is planning to publish a book she wrote based on guidance she received from him after he died.

I also did a reading for a woman whose son was shot in a drive-by shooting. When her son came to me in her reading, he told me she was burning candles for him by his picture on a stand beside her bed. When I told her that, she started crying, because that was exactly what she had been doing. The information confirmed for her that her son was alive in the spirit world and still aware of her. Here is a paragraph from a letter from her sister:

> *More than you know, the reading you gave in September for my twin sister, Kate, has reached far and wide, beyond my family to a larger community [of people] who are wounded and open to getting through their…pain by direction of the world of spirit. This has been a tremendous breakthrough. Thanks to you and to the world of spirit for that.*

Heart's Healing

The tragic thing, from my perspective, is that we don't experience the wholeness of ourselves, and we tend to identify too closely with our physical body and the traditional five senses. In actuality, we have *ten* senses—five physical senses and five spiritual senses—but most people are cognizant only of the physical senses. Even the concept of the spirit world is unfamiliar or alien to many. I find it hard to believe that a God of love created us with the intention that we should remain ignorant of the world of spirit and unable to communicate with the beings who live there. It doesn't make sense.

Humanity's spiritual awareness needs to be developed, step by step. We are spiritual as well as physical beings. With understanding, patience, and practice, it is possible for everyone to communicate with loved ones and spiritual guides and teachers on the other side.

Question: *I've looked at someone and thought I could swear the person was someone I knew who had passed away. My father has been dead for sixteen years, but sometimes I'll look in the rear* *view mirror of my car and see him or someone else whom I know to be dead. Can you explain what's happening in a case like this?*

Philip: Yes, I have had several experiences of seeing someone walking down the street and then disappearing into thin air! Spirit beings can materialize and then disappear. There are several stories of events like this in the Bible, as well as in contemporary spiritual writing.

Your father may indeed be trying to get your attention and encourage you to be aware of him through some of these experiences. He may wish to communicate with you. When that happens, listen! With faith say, "Dad, what do you want?" Speak and listen from your heart. The first thing that comes to you is usually the most accurate as to what a spirit is trying to convey.

It is also possible that your father's face or image is superimposed over a living individual, as spirit beings sometimes do that. When I give a presentation at a conference or even to a small group, I sometimes go into trance and serve as a channel for my master guide, Saint Germain, who uses my vocal cords to speak to people directly. He sometimes superimposes his own image over me and people who are clairvoyant see his face over my face. They also see a purple light around me, and that is his trademark.

What Are Near Death Experiences?

It's typical for people who have positive near death experiences to declare that they are no longer afraid of death. For them, the experience is a gift of grace.

Question: *A long time ago, I read a book about near death experiences called* After the Light *by Kimberly Clark Sharp. It included the story of a hospitalized woman who was declared dead. She saw her body below her and then moved high above the hospital, where she saw one sneaker on the ledge of an outside wall. When she was revived, she reported her experience. The hospital attendants thought she imagined all of this, until a nurse goes to the higher floor of the hospital and sees the sneaker on the ledge. What do you think about this?*

Philip: What happened to her is similar to experiences reported by many. As her physical body was undergoing great stress, her spiritual body rose to the vantage point from where she could see the shoe on that ledge. The brain resides with the physical body, but the mind resides with the spiritual body, so she was cognizant of everything that was happening to her. Hers was a real experience, and certainly important to her and to readers of the book.

If you could see your spiritual body clairvoyantly, you would find it looks just like you. It has a head, arms, and legs, and it is probably wearing clothing that appears just like what you are wearing. As I've said, you have five spiritual senses with which you can see everything in the spiritual and physical worlds. Your physical body is nothing more than a shell you will leave behind when you experience physical death. Think about a caterpillar in a cocoon. Through metamorphosis, the caterpillar leaves the cocoon and comes out as a butterfly.

If you think of this world as water and the spiritual world as air, you can sense the difference in the density of the two worlds. Because the spirit world is not as dense as this world, it vibrates at a higher frequency. To use our spiritual senses, we have to raise our vibration to the frequency level at which the spirit world exists, and most are not practiced at doing this. We even refer to the spirit world as the invisible world, but it is quite visible to our spiritual senses. We are just not accustomed to using them, so we don't see it, even though it interpenetrates this world. If we could use our spiritual senses, we would be well aware that we sometimes rise out of the physical body to have what some call "near death experiences."

Academic education gives us practical and intellectual training, but does not usually open our minds to the reality of the spirit world. Religions have various teachings about the world of spirit, but they have been fragmentary, conflicting, or fraught with fear and superstition. Science has come close to documenting spiritual reality, but because of bias or politics within the field, it's hard for scientists to work within a spiritually-aware framework. Because there has been no credible systematic information about them, our spiritual senses have tended to remain closed.

Some of us are born with a specific inclination and ability to use our spiritual senses, but we all have a certain something—intuition, a sixth sense, or a special knowing. Women seem to have it more than men, even if they are not fully aware of it. They use it in raising their children, or in sensing the dynamics among people.

Animals have natural sensitivity, too. This is why they react to changes in the weather and other situations before we are able to perceive what is happening.

Although we haven't realized it, a key to experiencing the spirit world is the proper use of the imagination. When children see a playmate who is not physically present, they may be seeing real people in the spirit world. Parents may think the right thing is to discourage them from using their imagination in this way, but it's usually a constructive experience. The important thing is to understand how children are affected by their interaction with unseen friends and try to ensure their experience is positive. It is never appropriate to simply deny the experience a child is having.

Question: *So many people who have near death experiences tell about a tunnel and a light. They have been told it's their imagination, a birth memory, or even a physical reaction within their brains. What do you think is actually happening to cause the specific impressions people have?*

Philip: The near death experience is an authentic spiritual experience, and people should be able to talk about it without feeling judged. It has been given to them to open their minds, alter their beliefs, or better prepare them and others to eventually pass into the spirit world.

The tunnel that many experience just represents a transition. People are going through an energy field to gain awareness of the spiritual world, not traveling across a physical distance. The process of transition from a physical awareness to a spiritual one is manifested through that sense of going through a tunnel.

Corresponding changes may also be occurring in the brain during near death experiences, but it's not correct that reported near death experiences are caused solely by the physical process of dying. One day scientists will broaden their understanding to include the spiritual world of cause as well as the physical world of effect. I realize that there are both cause and effect in the physical world, but in the grand scheme of things, the spirit world is the world of cause, and this physical world is the world of effect.

It's typical for people who have positive near death experiences to declare that they are no longer afraid of death. For them, the experience is a gift of grace. It is a particular kind of contact with the light of God and loved ones that is a vivid and life-changing experience for many.

This life and this moment are packed with the presence of spirit! Many of your relatives are standing by in great numbers right here with us. I am deeply touched by the presence of spirit in this room.

Can We Use Our Spiritual Senses to Understand Others?

We are drawn to people who accept us as we are. That's love.

Question: *When I attended Mass at my church some time ago, I sat next to a woman who was a complete stranger, and she said to me out of the blue, "I feel so much love coming from you that I just have to embrace you." Now, how would you explain that?*

Philip: Because you care for the dying, you probably register at a higher degree on the thermometer of love than the average person, and it shows in your eyes and in your face. In that religious setting, the spiritual aura of the woman sitting next to you was probably open, and because you were so close, your auras touched. That is why she responded as she did.

Question: *Can you tell us more about auras?*

Philip: There are many contemporary descriptions of auras, and historical examples include

Kirlian photography, thought to capture auras around leaves, and images of light around figures in art with religious themes. All of this relates to the same reality. In my experience, energy fields, or auras, exist around our bodies containing information about our essential nature, talents, and abilities, as well as our physical, emotional, or spiritual condition at a given moment. I consider myself a generalist in this area, because I don't go into a detailed analysis of auras in my work, but I often read auras for clients.

Question: *How do you actually read an aura? What do you see?*

Philip: I usually see more than one color in various combinations surrounding a person I'm reading for. I associate bright blue with an intellectual nature, certain shades of pink and light blue with very loving energy, and certain shades of green with healing abilities. When St. Francis appears in readings for clients he nearly always appears in a dark brown monk's robe. In this case, the dark brown is a reflection of his innate

Can We Use Our Spiritual Senses to Understand Others?

humility. Darker, less appealing shades of brown, black, or green might indicate illness or negative emotion, while dark red might represent anger or lust. A color indicating a problem may appear in a specific area rather than throughout someone's energy field. Nationality can be represented, as I see many people from India with at least some orange light, while most Americans have blue light around them. This is not absolute, but it is a general occurrence.

As I look at all of you, I think I would find that many of you have some basic colors in common. Because you work in the healing field, green might be a dominant color for you, and because of your service to others, I would not be surprised to see pink or light blue. If some of you are spiritually oriented, as I know you are, I am likely to see the color of indigo blue, and if you have practiced meditation for a length of time, your aura might include violet or gold.

Auras don't determine our nature or mood but reflect our essence and current behaviors, physical condition, or emotional state. We've all heard terms like "green with envy," "tickled pink," "feeling blue," or "seeing red," and we can feel the energy of anger if we walk into a room where people have had an intense argument. So the idea of sensing energy around someone or associating color with emotion isn't strange to most of us.

Reading auras is part of my gift of mediumship, and I usually do it soon after a reading begins. If, for example, I see bright orange light around an American, I'll ask if he has spent time in India, and the answer is usually yes. The accuracy with which I'm able to read auras tends to validate the entire reading for someone, and it helps me to know I'm being guided in the right direction for the person in front of me.

Question: Can you see auras around people all the time?

Philip: My spiritual senses are not open all the time, and I don't see auras around everyone I meet, though I often sense things about people. I see auras around people when I'm giving a spiritual reading because I have prepared for that.

[Addressing a woman in the audience] I have to smile as I say this, because I actually saw your

aura today when I walked in and sat down. I immediately thought, "This woman is psychic." One of my guides confirmed this by saying, "Yes, she has the potential to do the kind of thing you do." I could see that you were psychic by reading the energy field around you. Am I on track? *[Yes!]*

Question: *Does someone's aura tell you that you would or wouldn't want to know the person? Can you judge someone's personality or character by what you see in their aura?*

Philip: We all have an initial impression of whether we want to know someone better. When you sit next to a stranger at a movie theater, you sometimes feel uncomfortable and want to pull away. This is probably because the person's vibration or energy doesn't feel right to you. It's the same as when two different frequencies meet while dialing for a station on a radio, producing sound wave interference resulting in uncomfortable, shrill whining or squealing sounds. On the other hand, when you feel a higher vibration to which you are open, you are very drawn to it. You may be attracted to a person who has qualities you admire, strengths that complement your own, or a vibration that is similar to yours. You've all heard the expression, "We're on the same wave length."

Question: How can we use our spiritual senses to improve our day-to-day relationships?

Philip: We have an intuitive sense of people's energy, even if we don't see auras. We usually know when someone is angry or tense. We feel it. We are drawn to people who accept us as we are. That's love. Mothers have a sixth sense about the welfare of their children, and spouses read each other's moods.

The most important reason for developing spiritual sensitivity is to develop our ability to empathize. Sensing that a friend is going through a hard time helps us to reach out and offer a shoulder to lean on. When we understand that a co-worker is often moody, we are less likely to take it personally. If we come home to a tired spouse after work, a heightened awareness helps us to be supportive instead of becoming

Can We Use Our Spiritual Senses to Understand Others?

irritable ourselves. Sensing the energy around another person does help us in our relationships with others.

A final comment I would make is that spiritual sensitivity may tell us when a friend or loved one far away needs us. We may find ourselves thinking about a person or feeling drawn to make contact when we pray for someone. When we follow up on such feelings, it often validates what we were feeling and helps us to develop greater awareness as time goes by.

How Can We Deal with Fear and Negativity?

If you receive negative energy from someone, and you send out the positive energy of your love in return, you diffuse the negative energy and become free of it...

Question: *Toward the final days of their lives, some of our patients are afraid. Other than holding a hand, massaging a foot, speaking close to an ear, and doing whatever I can to make them physically comfortable, how can we help them deal with fear?*

Philip: Those who have lived with fear for a long time are often wedded to it, so it stays with them, even to the point of their departure into the spirit world. Our *understanding* about the world of spirit is the light that enables us to see things there. When people pass into the spirit world with no experience, knowledge, belief, or openness, they can't see things in their new environment, and they may find themselves initially in darkness. If they have lived a good life, however, even if they die in fear, people they were close to on earth will be there to assist them until they gradually understand. Let me share with you a passage from a book we published:

A man passed into the spirit world, believing in its existence, but without a clear understanding. He found himself in a misty darkness, like the last light of day. In the distance he saw a bright light and began walking toward it. He felt he was being guided to the light, though he couldn't see its source. As he drew closer, he realized that his brother, who had died several years before him, stood in the light, waiting for him. His brother guided him into the brighter light, and led him on from there.

It may be hard to give specific information about the spirit world to your patients, either because of their belief systems or because of hospice policies, but to the degree you are comfortable doing so, tell people that loved ones will be waiting for them on the other side. As I've said, this will help them see and experience the spirit world as they move into that reality.

Remember that you are not alone in your efforts to help. Those who wait on the other side to meet new arrivals have prepared for these events, and they have their own expertise

How Can We Deal with Fear and Negativity?

in helping people make the transition. You can also contribute to the welfare of your patients by praying for them if you are so inclined. Your prayers lend literal energy to all concerned as your patients go through the transition from life in this world to life in the spiritual dimension.

A dear friend passed away after a long struggle with breast cancer. Just before she died, her cousin was sitting beside her when she said, "Can't you hear them? They're talking about me. I don't know what they are saying, but I can hear them." Near the time when she took her last breath, she said, "Can you hear the music? It's so beautiful. Can you hear it?" There is always a point of separation when the spirit leaves the body. When people pass over, they gradually perceive more clearly those from the spirit world who have come to help them. Because of this attendance, they feel more at ease and are better prepared for their transition. Most of the souls who come from the spirit side to help are love itself. This love brings great reassurance and peace to those who are in the unfamiliar process of moving away from their physical existence.

Heart's Healing

It is a spiritual law that the degree of your love and the degree of your understanding about life determine the quality of your existence in the spiritual world when you leave your physical body. You can be religious in your beliefs, but if you haven't really loved others, you will be among religious people who aren't very loving. You will find yourself in the place that exactly reflects your level of love. If you really want to know who your neighbors will be in the spirit world, ask yourself these questions: What am I really like? How have I loved?

Question: On a practical level, how do you deal with negative energy when you feel it coming from someone?

Philip: The best way to deal with negative energy is to always give positive energy out, or as Jesus, said, "Love your enemies." Jesus said to forgive seventy times seven, not for the other person's benefit, but *your* benefit. What is the opposite? Bitterness, resentment, hatred, antagonism, and fear—all negative energies that will just keep you bound to that person. If you receive negative energy from someone, and you send out the positive energy of your love in return, you diffuse the negative energy and become free of it, because you have lifted yourself to a higher spiritual plane.

If you arrive in the spiritual world with extreme antagonism toward someone, it will draw you to the very person you don't want to see *or* be with! If someone has done something to hurt or malign you, and you are not able to let go of this, your grudge will hold you to that person. Hell or heaven is literally your state of mind in the spirit world.

Vivien: There is a story in one of the books we've published where a person in the spirit world was imprisoned in chains, bitterly hating the one he thought was keeping him in this state. What he couldn't see was that his "warden" was also chained. Finally, he was told by a higher being that no matter how much he could justify feeling resentful, unless he forgave this person, the links of the chains holding them together would never be broken. When he forgave the other person, he was immediately free.

Philip: The chain was a symbol of this man's anger and bitterness. During his physical life, he was in psychological chains that kept him strongly attached to the object of his resentment. In the spirit world, they became literal. He was bound to the one he hated by chains forged from his anger.

This story is from *A Wanderer in the Spirit Lands*, a book about someone's individual journey in the spirit world from darkness to light. It was in publication a number of years ago but has been out of print, and I felt the story was so valuable, we have re-published it. It's a primer about the spirit world which anyone can read without any special background knowledge, and it's also a wonderful love story. It illustrates the truth about many of the things we're discussing today.

The most important thing in life is love, and obtaining truth helps you know how to love. The two go hand in hand. As Dr. Raymond Moody said in his book, *Life after Life*, based on many cases of people coming back from near death or out of body experiences, the two things people are asked by those they meet on the other side

How Can We Deal with Fear and Negativity?

are: Have you learned? Have you loved? These are the two most important questions to ask of ourselves at any moment in our lives!

I am very practical. I have an agreement with my guides and teachers that I don't do my work out in the street, any more than a doctor would. I do my work in a sacred place when someone is with me for a reading in person or on the telephone. Otherwise, I have asked to be shut down, with some exceptions. When I am out in public, it would be painful and confusing to be spiritually open all the time.

I especially have a hard time at shopping malls when I am in an open state. It is very difficult because the central chakra, or energy center, is like a radar dish. When someone makes a loud noise, it hits you not in your ears or in your mind, but in your solar plexus chakra. Among crowds of people at shopping malls, there will be all kinds of motives and energies, so I either walk around with my arms across my solar plexus to protect myself, or I don't stay long. I also mentally place a white light around myself for protection. Thought energy is very real, and you can do the same thing.

Question: *Do you do this so that you won't be drained of your own energy?*

Philip: Yes, but also so that I won't accidentally be encroached upon by uncomfortable energies which some people carry with them.

I met with a client who had become a close friend. He called me from another country one day, and I didn't recognize his voice. It sounded the same physically, but the vibration he projected affected me in the solar plexus in an uncomfortable way. When he later came to see us, Vivien and I both sensed he had been invaded by a lower energy or spirit. This was not just our projection; it had really happened to him. It was disturbing to me, because I thought he had attained a certain strength and discipline of spiritual practice. I was unprepared to see such a change in him.

The influence of lower spirits causes a big percentage of mental problems. Certainly there are chemical imbalances, brain abnormalities, and traumatic experiences, but you could ask yourself, which came first?

How Can We Deal with Fear and Negativity?

Question: *How do you protect yourself from lower spirits? Do you do anything in addition to keeping yourself in a loving frame of mind and maintaining a positive attitude?*

Philip: The best course of action is always, whether or not you feel it, to try to project a loving attitude. When you are resolved to love actively, and you go about demonstrating that love, then true feelings of love will follow if they are not already there. If you say positive words, for example, positive energy will follow, and it will change the equation.

You must also protect yourself. You know the sayings, "Love your neighbor as yourself" and "God helps those who help themselves." As hospice workers, you know that you're really not any good to the person you're working with unless you are also integrated and happy with yourself. We all have to be mindful of this. I take the precautions that I do, because I am very open and receptive to the spirit world and energies tend to cling to me. I have learned the hard way that I have to protect myself. I have to work from the solar plexus area to send out nothing but the positive energy of love. Maybe I can help someone like my friend, but I have to protect and help myself in the process.

Be wary of teachings which say, "You must sacrifice yourself for others." If you are so busy with tasks for others that you don't take the time to know yourself, what are you sacrificing? When you truly know yourself, you can better understand and help others. The highest truth is to know yourself. When you do, you can understand and empathize with all humanity.

Vivien: We are attracted to people of a similar vibration. If you love others and maintain a high vibration, lower forces won't want to be near you. An example is that of an alcoholic who is constantly drawn to the bar. Spirits who were, and still are, addicted to alcohol also hover around the bars, hoping to vicariously experience drinking again through the alcoholics there. If a person isn't attracted to alcohol, he or she could go into a bar where those same spirits are and not be affected. The vibrations are so different, the spirits can't attach themselves.

Comment: *What you say ties into what psychologists say about body language—that when a person crosses his or her arms across the chest, this indicates the person is "closed." This is similar to the position you've described, with the arms crossed to protect the solar plexus area.*

Philip: Yes, I've read something about body language, and your example does seem to correlate with what I'm saying about how the physical body can be used to protect the solar plexus area.

The experiences I've had in readings also suggest a connection between psychological and spiritual reality. At the first reading I did for a woman I've read for more than once, I began with prayer and began to share information I was getting. Without knowing her profession, but because of what I was feeling, I asked, "Do you do some kind of counseling?" She replied, "How did you know that?" I said, "I see you sitting behind a desk, and I can tell by the energy level around you." Sometimes spirit will write out words in front of me to show what a person does, and sometimes they will give me symbols.

If there is a nurse, they may show me a nurse's cap above the person.

In any case, I said, "You're a therapist," and she confirmed this. Then I asked, "Do you use tarot cards in your work with patients?" Surprised, she asked, "How did you know that?" I said, "Because I can spiritually see them on your desk. Do you know who works with you to inspire you? Carl Jung. He has been guiding you for a long time." She said, "Oh my goodness! I wrote my master's thesis on Carl Jung. But if people in my profession knew I was using tarot cards, I'd be ridiculed."

Carl Jung then asked to step in and speak to this woman. He overshadowed me the way my master guide Saint Germain does during readings and sometimes speaking engagements. It was the only time I ever had this experience with him. He took over my voice and spoke directly to this woman, saying, "This is the wave of the future. Metaphysical and psychological approaches will come together, and then you will see real progress."

The work I am doing with you today is important—providing information about the

How Can We Deal with Fear and Negativity?

spirit world, according to your interests and questions. It is a great service to humanity and to those in spirit whenever we can bring the two worlds together with greater understanding. People *need* to hear information about the spirit world that validates their own experience. We should not keep our experiences to ourselves because we fear someone will reject them. If we put aside any stigma surrounding the spirit world, we can talk to each other about it as easily as we talk about the weather!

Does Meditation Help?

It is God who knows who you really are, and you can meet the living God by going inside.

Question: *Can you tell us about meditation and its relationship to the spirit world?*

Philip: Meditation is the act of sitting so still and relaxing so deeply that we enter what scientists call the "alpha state." In deep meditation, we can be in touch with our personal guides and teachers in the spirit world, often hearing or seeing them in our minds. As we learn to relax even more deeply, we realize we can be in touch with our real selves and with God, the creator of all. My experience is that prayer is how we speak to God, and meditation is how we listen.

Of greatest importance, meditation places us in a state where we are receptive to the love that is ever-available from God and the highest realms of the spirit world. We are always connected to this love, but in our busy lives we lose awareness of God's constant presence. Meditation brings us back into that awareness because our spiritual senses are more open in this state. Ultimately, we recognize that the love we encounter in mediation and prayer is the essence of who we are, and we are increasingly able to feel and express this in our daily lives.

We know very little about ourselves without *intentionally going inside*. That's the purpose and value of meditation. You have to go inside and become the observer of yourself, because your "you" is more than you think it is. It has been said that there are actually three of you: the person you think you are, the person other people think you are, and the real you! It is *God* who knows who you really are, and you can meet the living God by going inside. This may be a different approach to self-knowledge than what you are used to, but it's a true one.

Question: *You mentioned the "real" you. How can we bring that real person out in ourselves?*

Philip: The essence of who you are comes from the source of all life and light. You were created out of love, and your inner reality is love. The flip side of the coin of love is peace. Always

Does Meditation Help?

take the energy of love and peace toward any situation or person. The more you do that with other people, the more of your real self will come forth. That *is* your real self!

You are not this frantic man or that flustered woman. That's not the real you. When you pass into the spirit world, you will realize that you are light itself. You just can't see it now. You work with people *before* they pass over, and I work with them *after* they pass over. From my experience working with people on the other side, I can tell you without doubt what we look like there. *We are light!*

Question: *So how did we get into the position we're in? How did we become that frantic person, for example? Does this happen to us just through the everyday experience of living?*

Philip: We become this way because of the attachments we make to the physical world. Close your eyes and let's do an experiment. First, take three deep breaths and relax as much as you can:

You are on a river, in a beautiful golden boat, just lying back on some light green pillows. There is an oarsman, a very kind individual, rowing you along. You are so deeply relaxed under the warm sunlight. The birds are chirping and there is a slight breeze.

*You realize that all the things that are happening in your life are on the shore. As you move down this river, where are they? They are all being left behind you. What goes forward is the real you. That **you** is so important. That **you** is what you will take with you when you pass over into the spirit world. It is your essential character. It is your real self.*

As much as possible, don't be attached to the things of your life that cause you worry and stress. Leave them on the shore, as you move along on the river of life. Experience these things and learn from them, but let yourself keep moving past them. They are just a part of life. That's how it is. Think about it—how many of the things that you worry about never came to pass? The vast majority of them! So why waste your energy worrying? Put yourself in the hands

Does Meditation Help?

of love and peace, however you interpret that, but let it come out of your soul—out of the center of yourself.

Question: I have heard that meditation can be good for people with medical conditions. Do you know anything about that?

Philip: I don't have a medical background, but some who do are interested in the effects of meditation on blood pressure, stress management, and pain management. The National Institutes of Health has established a program to investigate the potential health benefits of meditation and practices such as acupuncture, hypnosis, and other less conventional approaches to health care.

Question: I am new to hospice work, and I haven't even done my training yet, but I have a question. I would like to think I don't, but if I'm honest, I really do have fears about death. Can I learn through meditation not to project fear to a person I'm working with?

Philip: As you overcome your own fear, you will not have to worry about projecting it to your

Heart's Healing

patients, and meditation can help. In my own experience, the more I meditate, the more certain I am that life is eternal and death is simply the doorway into the spirit world. I am able to visit that world now in prayer and meditation, and that gives me much certainty.

In case you or someone else here has not meditated before, I can make a few suggestions: First, there is no wrong way to meditate. Do what you can to set aside some regular time where you can be alone for however long you choose, from ten minutes to an hour. Sit in a comfortable position with your eyes closed and take some deep breaths to relax. Start by contemplating a word, image, or idea that brings you a feeling of peace, and observe your unfolding experience. It helps to keep a journal of your experiences, if this appeals to you, because more inspiration often comes through writing.

As you practice, you will find yourself connecting with a deeper reality; one that contains all love and all light. After a while, you may find that you can connect with this reality whenever you have a moment alone or even while walking to and from your car. This will help you feel greater peace about life and death, and you will be able to share that with your patients, just by being yourself. You will see forward movement on your spiritual path.

I also suggest reading as much material as you can about the reality of the world of spirit. We have a publishing company, and because of the level at which we work, in terms of our interests, we come across some wonderful books. *Closer to the Light* and *Saved by the Light* are two I'd recommend, and there is a book by Anthony Borgia called *Life in the World Unseen*. I have also written and published a number of books which might be helpful. Such books are worth reading, because they can inspire your confidence about what you'll experience when you arrive in the spirit world.

Once you have a sense of the reality of spirit world, through meditation and reading, and you know the beauty and love waiting for us there, your fear will rapidly diminish. You will have something of great value to share with your patients just by being present and available to listen with this understanding.

What Is Mediumship All About?

...We all have spiritual senses corresponding to our physical senses, and it is through our spiritual senses that we experience the world of spirit.

Question: *Could you share with us your early experiences as you awakened to this gift?*

Philip: I appreciate your question. As a child, I lived on a seventy-five-acre farm near Fort Wayne, Indiana, the third in a family of nine children. I was more reserved than many children, perhaps because I had more responsibility than most. My older brother and sister left home when I was twelve or thirteen, and since my father held down a full time job in the city, my mother needed help with the farm, housework, and taking care of my younger siblings. I learned much about life very early, and I'm deeply grateful for the experience.

When I had spare time, I spent it in the woods, walking and praying by myself. It was then that I had many encounters with the spirit world. Without prompting from anyone, I started praying for people of the world before I started school. I was so sensitive to others that when someone told me about something sad that had happened, my eyes would fill up with tears. I still feel physical pain when I hear of someone else's suffering.

I had many visitations from the spirit world during my childhood. One spirit being who came day and night was someone I knew as Brother Anthony, who I later learned was a fifteenth century German monk. He is always around when I'm working, and he is here right now. When I was a child, he came through to instruct me and sometimes guide me out of my body into the spirit world in preparation for the years ahead.

My mother came into my room some mornings to hear me relate how I had been visited by someone who stood by my bedside and spoke to me, and she told others about these visitors. My family didn't reject my early experiences, but they didn't understand enough to encourage me to continue to develop my awareness of the spirit world.

As I grew older, I was aware of fewer spiritual experiences, though I continued to have

What Is Mediumship All About?

profound dreams and visions throughout my adulthood. Finally, in my mid-forties, I decided to become a professional medium. I had visited another medium whose message pointed clearly and strongly in this direction; but it was not just the content of his message that convinced me. My own deeply positive response really got my attention! His message was simply the catalyst for my knowing what I wanted to do. I realize now that I was always attended by loving guides from the spirit world who inspired me up to and beyond that point to do just what I'm doing now. All of my experiences served to bring me into this work.

I'm not special. We're *all* being prepared for spiritual growth in this life and eventual entrance into the spirit world. We all have guides and teachers who support us in making a particular contribution to this world. For what purpose do they come? To help us learn and grow. Everyone has a part to fulfill toward helping to make this an integrated, functional world where our basic needs are met, and we can live together in peace.

Heart's Healing

Question: *What is the difference between being psychic and being spiritual?*

Philip: That's a great question. I don't consider myself solely a psychic or medium, because the foundation of my work is my relationship with God. While I come from the Christian spiritual tradition, I consider myself a mystic[1], and have a broad view about spiritual matters. I think the true religion of life is love. If we see religion as a way to connect with God or the divine, then for me, a loving person is a religious person.

I'm less concerned about my gift of mediumship than I am about the information I have learned and want to share. I find greatest fulfillment in helping people gain awareness about their true nature and the larger world of spirit, and I see my work is a bridge to this awareness. The time I spend in prayer and meditation is an important part of my ongoing spiritual develop-

---

[1] One who embraces a doctrine of direct communication or spiritual intuition of divine truth, or one who experiences a transcendental union of soul or mind with the divine reality or divinity. (Definitions are taken from *http://en.wiktionary.org/wiki/mysticism*)

ment, as it helps me to be more in tune with all that is beyond this physical plane.

I think of being psychic as having the mental ability to read thoughts, and an excellent example of this is extrasensory perception, or ESP. It's a gift that allows people to pick up thoughts, images, and ideas from someone else who is usually still on earth. Spiritual mediumship has more to do with communicating with those who live in the spirit world. I also think of spirituality as being centered more on love than on intellect.

As I've said, we all have spiritual senses corresponding to our physical senses, and it is through our spiritual senses that we experience the world of spirit. If you were to see clairvoyantly, you would see energy circling in each of seven energy centers or chakras located in specific areas of the body. Each one is associated with a certain color, but shades and patterns vary, depending upon the spiritual and physical condition of each individual.

The average person picks up impulses and vibrations primarily through the chakra, or energy center, located at the solar plexus, without being aware this is happening. Some actually have a kind of vision where they are unconsciously perceiving the spirit world.

The third eye is the center of spiritual sight, clairvoyance, where visual spiritual signals register. I call what happens when I receive these signals, "feel/see," because I actually feel or sense the information in my solar plexus as well as seeing a symbol or word or spiritual being that is coming through clairvoyantly to help me understand a message for someone. When I sit with a client and refer to a being who is there in spirit, I will often say, "I feel," but I'm not using the word "feel" in a typical sense. Once I tune in that way, I also begin to literally see clairvoyantly the spirit in front of me.

Question: Have you ever experienced automatic writing?

Philip: I worked with automatic writing for a while. As in any field, when you go into spiritual work, there are many areas from which to choose a specialization. In the field of nursing, you can be a surgical nurse or floor nurse. To really be good at anything, you have to narrow your focus. For this reason, I moved away from automatic writing.

One of my books is comprised of selected writings dictated through me by Saint Germain conveying information about the world of spirit. Saint Germain dictated most of the material. For a solid year, I got up at about 4:30 AM every Sunday and prayed in the same place each week. Saint Germain was present, walking back and forth, wearing a long purple robe. I could hear the material moving along the floor as he walked. He spoke to me and dictated words that I wrote down as I listened.

Sometimes, I could see a white light over my hand as I wrote, indicating his direct influence over my hand as well as my mind. In that sense, my experience in recording what Saint Germain wanted to get through was akin to automatic writing. When I read his dictation, I find it very beautiful writing, for which I can't really take credit, because of how it happened.

I don't do automatic writing on any consistent basis. There are people who have that expertise.

Over the next few years, you will find there is an increasing interest in spiritual matters. Why? The higher realms of the world of spirit are becoming more and more involved with our daily lives. When I first started this work, I was invited to talk about spiritual realities and experiences only in places where spiritual seekers gathered. Even so, only a few people really understood, and many were falling asleep! The fact that a spiritual medium is standing in a place of medical science, talking about life after death, is something no one would have imagined a short time ago!

What Happens During a Spiritual Reading?

The prayer is not a religious ritual, but a means of building the spiritual atmosphere and raising the vibration, centered on God. During the prayer, the energy around me starts changing, and the guides and teachers start coming through.

Question: How is a typical reading conducted?

Philip: I give written instructions before a scheduled reading to help people have the best possible experience. I ask them to send me a recent photograph with their handwritten full name and date of birth to give me a feeling of connection to their vibration as I prepare for the reading through meditation and prayer. I also ask them to write by hand and retain several questions about their most important concerns, and this handwritten information enhances my connection to each person during a reading.

As my meditation practice has developed, before each reading I now see in front of me, relatives, family members, friends, guides, teachers, and spiritual masters who gather for the occasion. It's my practice during the reading to tell the person who came and what they said. Mediums are lightning rods for everyone on

Heart's Healing

the spirit side who wants to come through. It is said that a good medium is like a telephone booth in the middle of Grand Central station at rush hour. Everyone gets in line and wants to use the phone!

When someone arrives, we sit together and pray or meditate for a short time, and I then ask to hold in my hand the tri-folded paper containing their handwritten questions, to better tune in to the spirit world around them. While I'm doing this, with my eyes closed, I go into a state of trance or semi-trance and give a general reading, often including a reading of the person's aura or energy field.

During the general reading, my guides often give responses to people's questions before I even know what they are. Without looking at their paper, I may say, "My guides tell me you have a question regarding a move," or "a problem with one of your children at school," and people will usually confirm this. Then I'll get further information, or the guide will ask me to have the question read aloud, which helps to focus the energy. I'll never look at the questions themselves, but hand the folded paper back to people

What Happens During a Spiritual Reading?

and ask them to begin reading their questions. Even though answers have often been given in the earlier part of the reading, additional information comes through. After forty-five minutes to an hour, I close with a prayer of gratitude.

I used to give most readings face to face, but because it is expensive for people to travel long distances for a one-hour reading, I now do most of them by telephone, and I have found this to be just as effective. I use a telephone headset and sit comfortably in a recliner with my feet up, so I can be very relaxed.

Because of my long experience, my vibration quickly becomes very peaceful, and I attain the proper receptivity, staying on that level while I am conducting the reading. As soon as a client calls, I open with prayer, as I would if we were meeting in person. The prayer is not a religious ritual, but a means of building the spiritual atmosphere and raising the vibration, centered on God. During the prayer, the energy around me starts changing, and the guides and teachers start coming through.

Four principal guides who work with me are in charge of bringing in different types of information or assisting a client's guides and loved ones to come through. One is a female and the others are male. Saint Germain usually stands to one side behind me, my guide Tiffany stands to my right, and Dr. Daniel David Palmer, the founder of chiropractic, stands to my left. My Indian guide, Black Hawk, walks around me to protect me from any unwelcome encumbrances. My guide Tiffany usually brings in symbols that help me, through my gift of mediumship, to decipher the answers to specific questions asked. As I am sitting there, she will whisper in my ear, or Saint Germain will touch me or talk in my left ear. Dr. Palmer will step forward if he has something to say or do. Black Hawk doesn't speak often, but he is always there to lend spiritual protection.

Does this all sound off the wall? I want you to know that it's very real to me, and I'll leave you to your own responses. There are hoaxes, and you'll read about them, but what I'm telling you about is the real thing.

Question: *Do you ever get information from the spirit world that you choose not to share?*

What Happens During a Spiritual Reading?

Philip: Yes. If I feel it is inappropriate for someone to hear certain information or the message is sensitive but unclear, I don't even bring it up. My goal is always to do no harm.

Question: What distinguishes your readings from one I might receive from another medium?

Philip: I have been a channel for the spiritual master Saint Germain for many years, and his work with me is an unusual aspect of the readings I give. With a voice distinctly different from mine, he actually takes over my vocal cords and speaks directly to people about their most important questions. More rarely, another spiritual teacher or someone very close to the person I'm reading for will overshadow me to the extent that my voice is slightly altered. During such experiences, I'm in a very deep trance and not aware of most of the information given.

Sometimes when I read for people, they experience being healed of physical pain. I presume that healing spirits take energy from me, although I don't know how this happens. At other times, I feel a pain or sensation that tells

Heart's Healing

me a person has a problem in that area. In the same way, I sometimes know the cause of someone's passing over. For example, I might know a spiritual being passed over because of a heart problem because I feel pain in the area of my heart. When I get this kind of information, it's usually confirmed by my clients.

According to reports from people I read for, it is during their direct experiences with Saint Germain that they are most likely to experience healing, and it can take place on a physical, emotional, or spiritual level. People say they feel extraordinary wisdom and love in Saint Germain's presence. Others who are clairvoyant have spoken about the intensity of purple and gold light that they see around me when Saint Germain comes through, and this indicates that he is a being from the highest realms of spirit.

Question: *Can the person you read for record the session?*

Philip: I make a recording of every reading and send a copy to the person the next day. After listening to the recording, people sometimes say there was much more information than they remember receiving. So much is given that it's hard to take it in during the reading itself. I do my best to give the maximum that time and energy allow.

Both the quality and quantity of information that comes through make each reading a uniquely moving experience, and many people want to come back for more. My readings are by appointment, and the calendar usually stays quite full. I do ask people to wait at least three months before scheduling another reading because I don't want them to become dependent on me or on messages from the other side. Also, they will not be able to put all of the information to use in a shorter interval. Any of us needs time to assimilate new understanding and apply it to our lives before we are ready for more.

Question: *Do you have any advice on questions people should ask in a reading?*

Philip: The questions should come out of your own soul. I tell people not to ask for information they can get on their own. You have common sense and can use your own brain to get many answers for yourself. There is always a world of spirit around you, and you can ask your own guides and teachers for guidance in choosing your questions. People go to mediums, in most cases, to receive information they can't get from anyone else.

On the other hand, any question is all right as you may need confirmation of something you already feel to be true. No matter what you ask, your guides know the answers you need at this time in your life, and they usually find a way to bring that information through, in a general message, or in response to one of your questions.

Vivien: People often ask about marriage, children, health, or the direction of their careers. Sometimes you feel as though you are going through a big transition in your life, and you have a sense of what you want to do, but you aren't sure. At such times, a reading will help to clear things up or confirm what you are thinking or planning.

Philip: Sometimes I can see that a client is going to move, and even where they are going—at least the general area. That's an example of information that may validate a decision someone is trying to make.

One of the most important questions, which people often don't think to ask, is this: "Can you give me any information about my spiritual path?" This is the question you will be asking at the end of your life. What kind of life did I live? This is also a question many of your patients may be asking.

Question: Have you ever been to a medium yourself?

Philip: I periodically check in with other mediums who have a track record of being credible and accurate, so I can receive validation for the guidance I receive. It helps me to stay on my path and remain in proper alignment with heaven. I have used the services of several mediums who usually have not known me or my work. I do this so that I receive the most objective information possible.

Question: What are some experiences you have had during the readings you have given?

Heart's Healing

Philip: As I've said, each reading is unique, not always because of spiritual phenomena, but because of the love that is shared between the spiritual being coming through and the person who is there to receive messages. I will share a few memorable experiences:

In one reading, Paramahansa Yogananda, the Guru who introduced Kriya Yoga to the west, suddenly came through, surrounded by a brilliant orange light. Orange is the color often associated with him, and the light also surrounded the woman I was reading for. I felt his love for her so strongly that I started to cry. I could literally *see* the love come in, and it was so sweet that I couldn't stop crying. Then he removed from his head the turban he was wearing and said, "Tell her I'm giving this to her." Because of this powerful appearance, I assumed she must be associated with him in some way, so after I recovered enough to speak, I asked, "Do you know Yogananda?" She laughed and said that she and her husband had been the leaders in a center for his teachings in their locality for many years.

What Happens During a Spiritual Reading?

Hippocrates has been in the spirit world for a long time, so he came in to one of my readings with a blinding white light. The experience affected me deeply, and I had to stop the reading for a moment just to get back my equilibrium. Hippocrates spoke to me about the woman I was reading for, giving a substantial message about her profession. Only after the reading was over, she said, "You know, Hippocrates is my guide. Last night, I was out walking and I asked him about one of the questions I had written down on that paper. He gave me the same answer last night that you brought through today!"

I said earlier that when I was a child, I received frequent bedside visits from a fifteenth century monk I called Brother Anthony. Only my wife knew about him. At one point I attended a meeting in Pennsylvania where people were receiving spiritual messages. The person leading the group was talented in physical mediumship, a rare practice these days, and while we were there, we saw extraordinary physical manifestations of spirit. All of those present heard voices of various spirits speaking through megaphones suspended in air, and we saw spirit beings gradually materialize out of thin air into full bodily form.

The most moving experience for me was the full bodily materialization of my old friend, Brother Anthony. He appeared in solid form, totally animated and alive, wearing a white robe and hood. While he gave a blessing to all of us as we sat in a circle, the medium said he had come specifically for me and his name was "Brother Anthony." The medium knew nothing about my early childhood visitations, and I had not thought about them for a long time. I was humbled and amazed when he appeared in that setting.

I've seen Gandhi appear in the same way. He came to a friend of ours who had always loved his teachings and example. He came out in earthly form, took her by the arm, and walked with her.

How Can We Know What Messages to Trust?

Truth is truth, however you approach it. If everything is energy, then everything is real.

Question: *How can you validate what you are told by someone who claims to be a medium? I have a big problem with people who try to be mediums without any real understanding, and I think this can be dangerous for the people who listen to them.*

Philip: I agree with you. There are people who are spiritually open who see or hear spirit without much understanding or direction, and they may speak with little wisdom or care about what they see. They may also give information that is shaded by their own belief system. That is true for anyone to an extent, but I exercise great care not to give too much interpretation about what I am shown. It's much better to tell people what I see and let them take responsibility for determining what it means and what to do with it. I have also asked my guides to give me true information that is encouraging and helpful to the person I am reading for. I never want to give information that may do more harm than good, even if it *is* true.

Your comment is quite important. To avoid the pitfalls you mentioned, I went through rigorous training with one of the best mediums in the United States who has done credible readings for many people. Mediums must guard against the projection of their own thought energy out in front of them. They may be witnessing their own subjective projection, believing that they are reading it as objective information.

The responsibility for "quality assurance" lies both with the medium and the person who comes for a reading. The medium must do everything possible to be prepared to give accurate, objective information with the intent of helping someone to progress on their own spiritual journey. People who come for a reading must be intellectually and emotionally prepared to apply the information in a responsible way for their own highest good. This is yet another reason why people need to understand the reality of the spirit world and learn to use their own spiritual senses to distinguish between the vibration of wisdom from a higher plane and that of information that carries little or no meaning for them.

I do not claim perfection in my ability to give readings. No one is perfect, and mediums are human beings who have on and off days, like everyone. I think the accuracy of most mediums is, at best, eighty-five to ninety percent. Sometimes it's higher if a medium is in trance, because this helps to reduce the potential influence of the medium's own thoughts and feelings and provides spirit beings with more direct access to the client. An example of this is when Saint Germain channels through me and uses my vocal cords to speak directly.

I advise people to consider whether or not the essence of what comes through is true and to be mindful that those from the world of spirit are trying to get through a vibration that can be denser than a wall for them. They must get information through first to me and then to the person with whom they want to communicate. Sometimes the atmosphere is so dense that the information coming through may be distorted, or I may not hear or see the message correctly every time. I do the best I can do, given the limitations within which I sometimes work.

Question: *What is your opinion about the teaching of reincarnation?*

Philip: For years, I believed that there was no such thing as reincarnation. As an alternate theory, based on information from my guides and my own observations, I concluded that some spirits passed their thoughts and beliefs to people on earth who interpreted this information to mean that they were the current embodiment of that spirit.

What I think now is that I don't really know. So I suggest to people that the best thing to do is just to live a good life. That's the important thing. In either case, you don't want to repeat your steps in this life, either by having to come back in spirit to try to influence people on earth through their minds, or by coming back as a baby and having to live the cycle of physical life all over again. Whatever is true about this question, this life is about progressing on the spiritual path. If we act in accordance with that understanding, we will be in good shape when we pass over.

Question: *Do we have spiritual experiences when we dream?*

Philip: Some dreams are thought energy or images left over from remembrances of the day, or an earlier time. But some dreams are spirit visitations. You can learn to tell the difference. I'll give you an example: A woman's baby dies, and she grieves deeply over the loss. In a dream, she goes to where the baby is, holds and comforts him, talks to him, and talks to others around them. The colors in the dream are vibrant and the images are clear. There is no inconsistency or confusion in the sequence of events, and she feels the substantial existence of her child as she holds him. When she awakens, her grief has lessened.

Did this woman have a dream or a spiritual experience? She may well have been helped by higher beings to actually go to the place where the baby was and spend time with him. Both in the dream and after she awakened, the mother could sense that her baby still lived, albeit in another dimension of reality, and she took great comfort from the close contact she felt with her child once more.

The rigorous skeptic may say it was all in the woman's subconscious mind, and therefore not real. How can we know? Sometimes I think the argument between science and religion is beside the point. Truth is truth, however you approach it. If everything is energy, then everything is real. We know this mother had a precious and positive experience that was more than real to her.

Question: *Many years ago I read Jane Roberts' books about Seth, and what I read seems similar to what happens with you. I don't know how you feel about Jane Roberts and don't even know if she's still alive, but I'm sure Seth is! What do you know about him?*

Philip: The important thing about a spiritual book is not the exact content, but whether it helped open you up to higher understanding. If it did that, then it served its purpose. Many such writings serve that higher purpose.

Vivien: There are many teachers from the world of spirit coming today through different sensitives, and they are all raising our consciousness. A certain spiritual messenger may be better suited to one person than another.

Philip: Where trust is concerned, the most important person to trust is yourself. Through the practice of prayer and meditation, going inside to sincerely ask questions and listen for guidance, you are likely to stay on the right track. We are all on the same path leading to God, but everyone is on a different point in the journey, causing us to see things differently along the way. Wherever we are, the important thing is to keep moving forward, guided by our desire for love and truth, and trusting our inner compass for direction. Jesus said, "Seek and you will find," and I believe that is true.

Your work and mine are very different, but we are all in the business of healing. While your mission is to comfort rather than cure, you bring a healing touch in all that you do with patients.

Heart's Healing

My mission is to teach others about the spirit world and life after death, but I work constantly with healing energies that come through me from the other side.

Some who come to me for readings say they experience physical healing, but many more say they experience emotional or spiritual healing. One person put it best: After her reading, she said she had never felt so understood and so loved, because the elevated spirit beings who came through seemed to know everything about her, outwardly and inwardly, and love her all the more for seeing her so clearly. This helped her to feel compassion and forgiveness for herself, and she shed tears of gratitude and relief. To me, this healing of the heart is more important than physical healing. Why is this?

The heart's healing brings us the ability to love ourselves, making it possible for us to genuinely love others. Forgiving ourselves, we forgive others. Understanding ourselves, we understand others. We are all going to die, and we will leave the physical body behind, but we will not leave love behind.

From my perspective, your helping individuals in their transition from a physical to a spiritual life, is a most sacred service. You are in the place where you can see, understand, and love the people you serve. In the days and weeks before their passing, you provide physical healing and comfort through various treatments, emotional healing through empathy and encouragement, and spiritual healing through compassion, which expresses the very nature of God. Doctors delivered your patients into the world, and in many ways, you are delivering them into the world of spirit. Your comfort and aid at this momentous time of their lives will never be forgotten by them or by those waiting on the other side to receive them. Your loving attendance to a dying patient is a very special, eternal gift that you give.

Your thoughtful questions have made our time together a very rewarding experience for me, and I hope you feel you have gained something from our exchange. It has been a privilege to be here with you, and I wish you all of life's richest blessings.

Hospice

In the minds of many, the word *hospice* is associated with compassion, competence, comfort, and a holistic concept of care for those near the end of life. Hospice provides medical, social, and emotional support for patients and families, including pain management and bereavement counseling. Spiritual counseling is available for those who want to explore their own convictions and hopes relating to end of life decisions and life after death. Hospice services are provided primarily in the home, but can be delivered in care facilities as needed. In the United States, fees are usually covered by public and private insurance plans.

Origins of the hospice concept can be traced back to eleventh century shelters for sick or weary travelers, but it was not until the 1950s that the modern concept of hospice care was developed in England. The first hospice in America was founded in 1974, and today hospice care is delivered in communities throughout the world. In its 2009 edition of "Hospice Care in America," the National Hospice and Palliative Care Organization reported that in 2008, an estimated 1.45 million people received care in 4,850 hospice programs located in all 50 states, the District of Columbia, Puerto Rico, Guam, and the U.S. Virgin Islands.[2]

---

[2] *http://www.nhpco.org/files/public/Statistics_Research/NHPCO_facts_and_figures.pdf*

Mastery Press

Phoenix, Arizona

For general inquiries send an email to
PB@PhilipBurley.com or write to:

Adventures in Mastery, LLC (AIM)
P.O. Box 43548
Phoenix, AZ 85080

For more information about Philip Burley
and the work of
Adventures in Mastery, LLC,
please visit this website:
www.PhilipBurley.com